This book is dedicated to my daughter Emily, and my son Alexander. May the joy of childhood last a lifetime.
Love Always, Mom

Copyright ©, Penny S. Dodson 2022

There are facts that we all know about Santa:

1. He lives in the North Pole

2. Santa is married to Mrs. Claus

3. Santa wears a red suit

4. Reindeer pull Santa's sleigh

5. Elves help Santa build toys

6. Santa delivers toys on Christmas Eve

Santa has one job and he knows how to do it.
Santa is already prepared for the holiday season.

Santa wanted to go on vacation with his wife before the holidays. It was time for an adventure.

Santa and Mrs. Claus talked about the kind of activity they would like.
Should they go hiking in Patagonia?

Or snowboarding in Colorado?

One year Santa and Mrs. Claus took a vacation to beautiful Hawaii. While in Hawaii they enjoyed delicious fresh pineapples.

After relaxing on the beach, they took surf lessons.

Then Santa remembered an event he had heard about in California. Every year, in a California beach town called Dana Point there was a Surfing Santa Contest!

That was it, they had decided! A California surf trip would be a great vacation. They started planning their beach getaway.

They were ready to get back to the beach.
The elves made Santa and Mrs. Claus
custom surfboards.

Santa usually only wears his Santa Suit during the Christmas season. The rest of the year he dresses like everyone else. Sometimes he is recognized. Santa just smiles, he is happy to bring joy to others.

In this surf contest everyone is dressed as Santa. So he will blend in with the other surfers there.

After Santa and Mrs. Claus packed everything they needed for their trip into the sleigh they were ready to go.

When Santa leaves the North Pole, he flies in his sleigh.

After the flight they checked into the hotel that they booked. The hotel was beautiful and it had an ocean view.

The next day was the surf contest. They ate dinner at a restaurant. After dinner they quickly went to sleep.

They woke up early the next morning. The Surfing Santa event started at 7: OO a.m.

They ate some oatmeal and fruit for breakfast. Then they walked down with their surfboards to the beach.

Even in a crowd of Santa's at the beach, people were still looking at Santa because of his thick white beard. He saw two children whispering as he walked by, "do you think that's really him?" Santa smiled and wished them both a good morning. They looked surprised and then they both smiled and said, "good morning Santa!"

Santa and Mrs. Claus had a great day at the event.
It was fun to see all the Santas' in the ocean
and on the beach.

Santa learned that money raised from the event went to help children with autism.

"What a wonderful day," Santa said. "What a great event," said Mrs. Claus. They were both happy that they got to surf and help children too.

They went back to the hotel to clean up and pack. Their sleigh would be picking them up soon to fly back to the North Pole.

The next morning they told everyone
they could about their surf trip.

Everyone was excited and they all talked about going as a group together next year.

So, when you go to the beach, if you see someone dressed like Santa Claus,
be sure to wave or say "hello."

Made in the USA
Columbia, SC
01 December 2022

72375780R00020